Countries and Cultures

Afghanistan

by Mary Englar

Content Consultant:
Dr. Maliha Zulfacar, Ethnic Studies Department
California Polytechnic State University
San Luis Obispo, California

Reading Consultant:
Dr. Robert Miller, Professor of Special Populations
Minnesota State University, Mankato

Capstone press

Mankato, Minnesota

Capstone Press
151 Good Counsel Drive, P.O. Box 669, Mankato, MN 56002
http://www.capstone-press.com

Copyright © 2004 by Capstone Press. All rights reserved.
No part of this publication may be reproduced in whole or in part, or stored in a retrieval system, or transmitted in any form or by any means, electronic, mechanical, photocopying, recording, or otherwise, without written permission of the publisher. For information regarding permission, write to Capstone Press, 151 Good Counsel Drive, P.O. Box 669, Dept. R, Mankato, Minnesota 56002.
Printed in the United States of America

Library of Congress Cataloging-in-Publication Data
Englar, Mary.
   Afghanistan / by Mary Englar.
   v. cm.—(Countries and cultures)
   Includes bibliographical references and index.
   Contents: Explore Afghanistan—Afghanistan's land, climate, and wildlife—Afghanistan's history and government—Afghanistan's economy—Afghanistan's people, culture, and daily life.
   ISBN 0-7368-2174-0 (hardcover)
   1. Afghanistan—Juvenile literature. [1. Afghanistan.] I. Title. II. Series.
DS351.9.E54 2004
958.1—dc21   2003002654

Summary: Discusses the geography, history, economy, and culture of Afghanistan.

Editorial Credits
Gillia Olson, editor; Heather Kindseth, series designer; Molly Nei, cover and interior designer; Alta Schaffer, photo researcher; Karen Risch, product planning editor

Photo Credits
Cover photos: Koh-i-Baba Range, Corbis/Ric Ergenbright; woven textile, Doranne Jacobson

Art Resource, 22; Art Resource/Giraudon, 18; Bruce Coleman Inc./John Elk III, 56; Bruce Coleman Inc./John Giustina, 17; Capstone Press/Gary Sundermeyer, 53; Corbis/Paul Almsay, 8; Corbis Sygma/Zaheeruddin/Webista, 21; Cory Langley/Teressa Rerras, 1 (left, middle), 4, 44, 51; Doranne Jacobson, 11, 12; Gayle Zonnefeld, 40; Getty Images, 34, 63; Getty Images/Hulton Archive, 25, 26, 29; Getty Images/Paula Bronstein, 55; Getty Images/U.S. Army/Sgt. Edward Zink, 33; John Elk III, 1 (right); One Mile Up, Inc., 57 (both); TRIP/E. Parker, 31; TRIP/H. Leonard, 48; TRIP/M. Lines, 47; TRIP/R. Zampese, 43; Victor Englebert, 36

Artistic Effects
Corbis; Flat Earth; PhotoDisc, Inc.

1 2 3 4 5 6 08 07 06 05 04 03

Contents

Chapter 1
Fast Facts about Afghanistan 4
Explore Afghanistan 5

Chapter 2
Fast Facts about Afghanistan's Land 8
Afghanistan's Land, Climate, and Wildlife 9

Chapter 3
Fast Facts about Afghanistan's History 18
Afghanistan's History and Government 19

Chapter 4
Fast Facts about Afghanistan's Economy 36
Afghanistan's Economy 37

Chapter 5
Fast Facts about Afghanistan's People 44
Afghanistan's People, Culture, and Daily Life 45

Maps
Geopolitical Map of Afghanistan 7
Afghanistan's Land Regions and Topography 15
Afghanistan's Industries and Natural Resources 39

Features
Snow Leopard 17
Afghanistan's Money 40
Learn to Speak Pashto 51
Recipe: Make Khatai Cookies 53
Afghanistan's National Symbols 57
Timeline 58
Words to Know 60
To Learn More 61
Useful Addresses 62
Internet Sites 62
Index 64

Fast Facts about Afghanistan

Official name: Dowlat-e Eslami-ye Afghanestan (Islamic State of Afghanistan)
Location: southern Asia
Bordering countries: China, Pakistan, Iran, Tajikistan, Turkmenistan, Uzbekistan
National population: 27,755,755
Capital: Kabul
Major cities and populations: Kabul (1,780,000), Kandahar (226,000), Herat (177,000), Mazar-e Sharif (131,000), Jalalabad (58,000)

Chapter 1

Explore Afghanistan

For thousands of years, the Khyber Pass has brought opportunities and problems to Afghanistan and neighboring countries. The pass was the easiest way through the mountains between Afghanistan and Pakistan. People from all parts of Asia and Europe traded goods along this route. This constant movement of people left Afghanistan with a diverse population of ethnic and tribal groups that speak more than 70 different languages. This easy crossing point also allowed conquering armies to attack Afghanistan and its neighboring countries.

The Khyber Pass is about 33 miles (53 kilometers) long. Today, it allows people to travel from Peshawar, Pakistan, to Kabul, Afghanistan. Passing through the mountains, the pass narrows to 42 feet (13 meters) at one point. It reaches an elevation of 3,500 feet (1,067 meters) at the border between Afghanistan and

◀ The Khyber Pass cuts through the Safed Koh Mountains between Pakistan and Afghanistan.

Pakistan. Two roads wind along the pass. One is paved for vehicles, and the other is a dirt track used by travelers with horses, donkeys, and camels.

Landlocked

Afghanistan is a landlocked country located in southern Asia. It shares no border with the sea. Its land borders include Iran on the west and Pakistan on the south and east. On the north, the Amu Darya River divides Afghanistan from the central Asian countries of Tajikistan, Uzbekistan, and Turkmenistan. Afghanistan also shares a short border with China in the northeast. Afghanistan covers about 250,000 square miles (647,500 square kilometers), an area about the size of the U.S. state of Texas.

Since 1979, Afghanistan has been a place of conflict. In 1979, the former Soviet Union invaded, trying to keep communism alive in Afghanistan. Meanwhile, the United States trained Afghan fighters to combat the Soviets to try to stop communism. The Afghans succeeded in pushing out the Soviets in 1989. The Afghans then fought among themselves for the right to govern Afghanistan. In 2001, after the terrorist attack of September 11, the United States sent troops into Afghanistan to help Afghan groups topple the ruling Taliban. Today, the Afghan people, with the help of the international community, are struggling to overcome the last 25 years of conflict.

Geopolitical Map of Afghanistan

KEY
- ✪ Capital
- • City

7

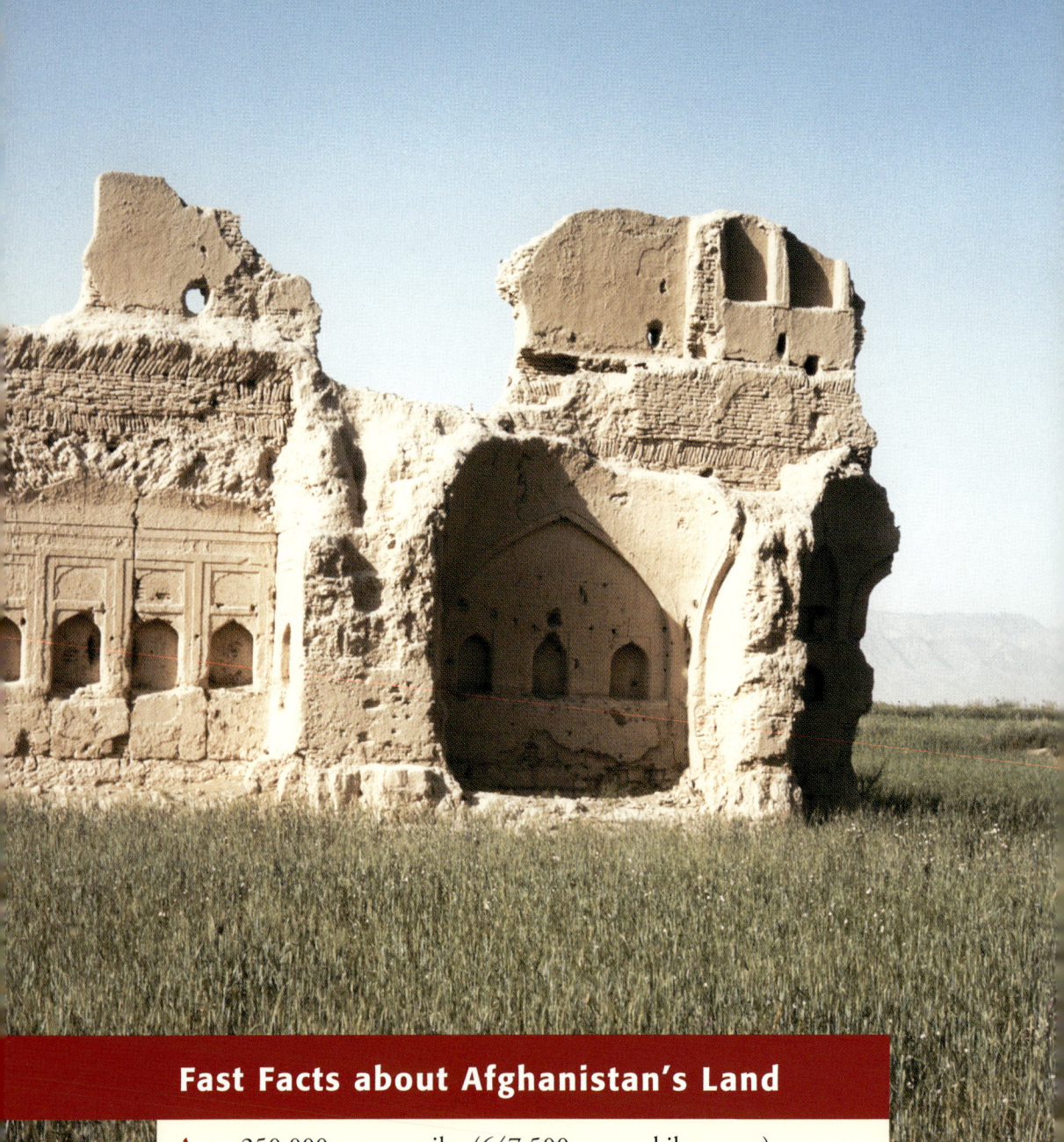

Fast Facts about Afghanistan's Land

Area: 250,000 square miles (647,500 square kilometers)
Latitude and longitude: 33 degrees north latitude, 65 degrees east longitude at Afghanistan's geographic center
Highest elevation: Nowshak, 24,557 feet (7,485 meters)
Lowest elevation: Amu Darya River, 846 feet (258 meters)

Chapter 2

Afghanistan's Land, Climate, and Wildlife

Mountains dominate Afghanistan's landscape, covering more than 60 percent of the country. These mountains divide the country into three different regions. They are the northern plains, the central highlands, and the southwestern plateau.

Northern Plains

The small northern plains region contains most of the country's farmland. The area receives only 7 inches (18 centimeters) of precipitation per year, making irrigation essential to farming. The Harirud and Qonduz Rivers are vital to these irrigation systems. The Amu Darya River is also lined with farmland. Most of the rivers in northern Afghanistan empty into the Amu Darya. Much of the northern plains region is covered with grasslands where farmers bring livestock to graze.

◀ The ruins of this building from the A.D. 1000s stand at Balkh in the northern plains region.

Mazar-e Sharif is sometimes called the "gateway to the plains." This city lies near the southern edge of the plains. It is one of the country's largest and oldest cities. It lies along ancient trade routes.

Central Highlands

The central highlands region is made up of the Hindu Kush Mountains and its foothills. This mountain range is a continuation of the mountains of the Himalaya. High peaks above 20,000 feet (6,100 meters) are common in northeastern Afghanistan. Kabul (KAH-buhl), Afghanistan's capital and largest city, is located in the Hindu Kush.

The harsh landscape of high peaks and narrow valleys makes crossing the mountains difficult. The Salang Pass between Kabul and the northern plains is 11,033 feet (3,363 meters) at its highest point.

Many rivers start in the highlands region. The Kabul River leads to the sea, but only through the Indus River of Pakistan. The Helmand River is Afghanistan's longest inside its borders. The Arghandab River flows into the Helmand.

The colorful Band-e Amir Lakes lie in the middle of the central highlands. These lakes spill over from one to the next. Their colors range from white to brilliant blue to green.

▲ People farm in the valleys between mountains in the central highlands region.

The central highlands region often has earthquakes. In the last 100 years, more than 70 major earthquakes have hit Afghanistan.

Southwestern Plateau

The southwestern plateau region covers slightly more area than the northern plains. This land is mostly dry,

▲ Nomads trek across the dry southwestern plateau region.

12

rocky desert. The Registan Desert covers one-fourth of the plateau. This desert has sand dunes as high as 100 feet (30 meters).

The Helmand River flows from the highlands through the plateau region to Lake Helmand. Lake Helmand lies in a large, marshy area on the border with Iran called the Sistan Basin. Lakes in this area have very salty water.

Kandahar is located in the southwestern plateau region. This city was once the capital of Afghanistan. Currently, it is the country's second largest city.

Climate

Afghanistan has cold winters and hot, dry summers. Winter lasts from December to April, while summer lasts from May to November. Cold weather brings rain in the low elevations and snow in high elevations.

Overall, Afghanistan is a dry country. The amount of precipitation does differ slightly by region. Mazar-e Sharif in the northern plains receives an average of 8 inches (20 centimeters) of precipitation each year. Kabul, at an altitude of 5,900 feet (1,800 meters), receives an average of 11 inches (28 centimeters) of rain and snow each year. The desert of the southwestern plateau receives as little as 3 inches (7.6 centimeters) of rain each year.

Few records have been kept of average daily temperatures in Afghanistan. Only Kabul has a good record of average temperatures. Kabul averages 75 degrees Fahrenheit (24 degrees Celsius) in July, and 25 degrees Fahrenheit (minus 4 degrees Celsius) in January. The lowest temperature ever recorded in Kabul in winter was minus 24 degrees Fahrenheit (minus 31 degrees Celsius).

Plant Life

The dry climate throughout Afghanistan limits the variety of plants found there. Low bushes called scrub grow in the desert. Shrubs and bushes such as currant, honeysuckle, hawthorn, and gooseberry live on the foothills and plains. If enough rain falls in the spring, grass and wildflowers cover the plains.

At one time, most of the eastern mountains were covered with forests. Afghanistan's ongoing wars have contributed to deforestation. Army soldiers cut down trees to build fires. Refugees in camps cut down trees and shrubs for firewood to cook their meals. It is estimated that only 2 percent of Afghanistan remains forested. These forests are in the northeast mountains.

Wildlife

In the past, Afghanistan was home to a large variety of animals. Siberian tigers were found along the Amu Darya River in the north. Antelope and gazelles roamed the deserts. More than 380 species of birds

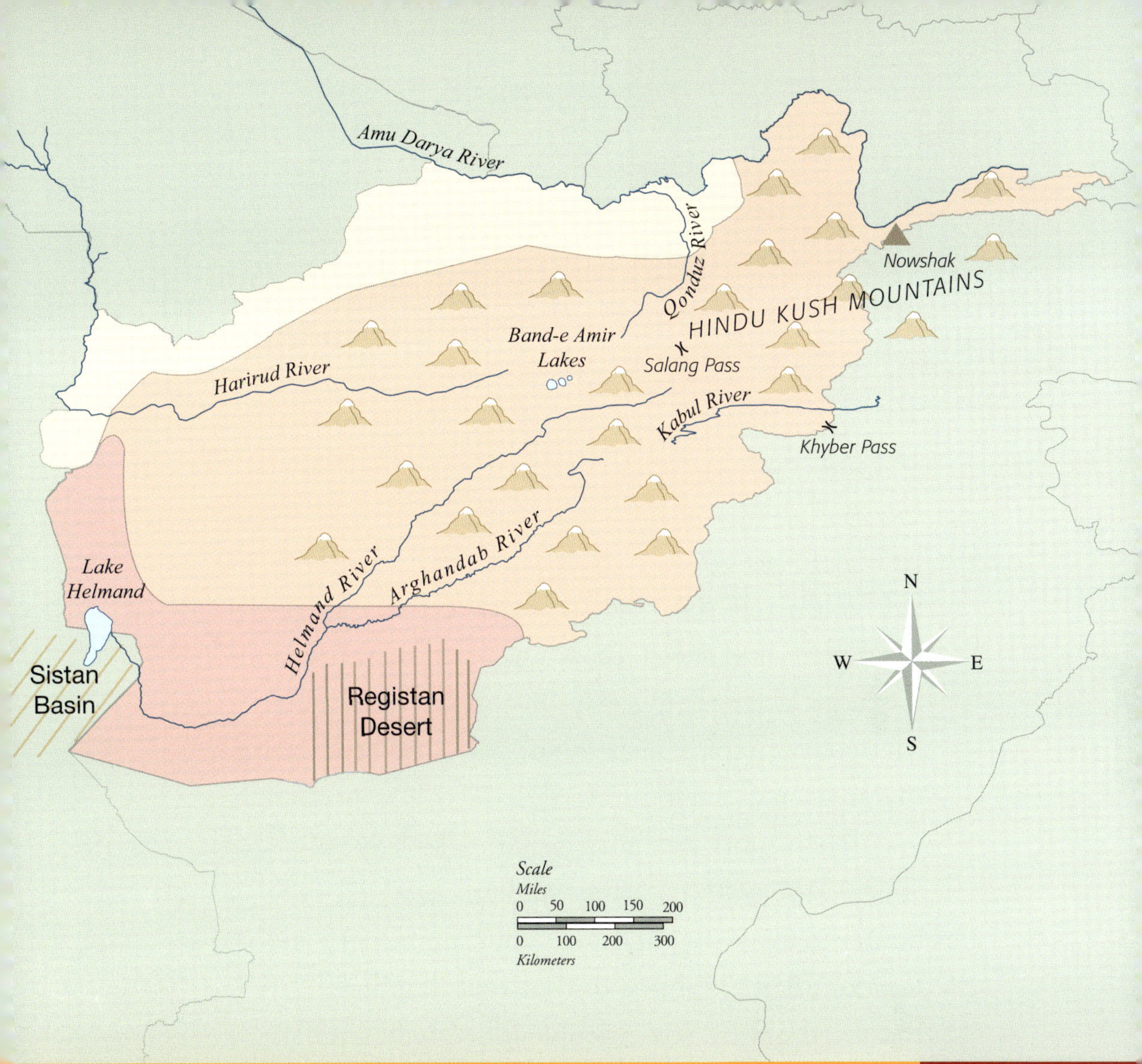

Afghanistan's Land Regions and Topography

KEY
- Northern Plains
- Central Highlands
- Southwestern Plateau
- ▲ Mountain
- Mountain Range
- Mountain Pass
- Basin
- Desert
- River

15

> **Did you know...?**
> Afghan hounds originally developed in southern Asia. Afghans used them to help hunt game in the mountains.

were reported, either migrating through Afghanistan or nesting there. After years of drought and war, no one is sure how many animals remain.

Some animals can be found in the remaining forests and high in the mountains. People have seen wolves, foxes, otters, lynx, hyenas, and jackals. Experts believe the rare snow leopard lives in the northeast. Wild goats and sheep, including ibex, markhor, and the large Marco Polo sheep, live in the mountains. Mongooses, moles, hedgehogs, bats, and other small mammals may be found in areas with few people.

Afghanistan's wars and droughts have greatly affected the wildlife. Many Afghans have left their homes to avoid the fighting. They are hungry and hunt animals and birds to feed their families. During the wars, some people killed wild animals and traded the fur for food.

In February 2002, the United Nations announced it would survey the damage to land, crops, water sources, and animals for the first time since the late 1970s. The Afghan people know that they must replant their forests and croplands for the animals, land, and people to recover.

Snow Leopard

The highly endangered snow leopard is found at high elevations in the mountains of Central Asia. Scientists estimate that fewer than 100 of these wildcats survive in the mountains of Afghanistan.

The snow leopard is well suited to its habitat. Its thick, gray fur is spotted with dark gray "pawprints" that help it blend into the rocky mountain areas. Its tail is almost as long as its body. The tail helps the leopard keep it's balance when it leaps through rocky terrain.

The leopards are solitary animals. Except when mothers have cubs, they live and hunt alone. They prefer to eat wild sheep and goats, but they will also eat rabbits and birds. On this meat diet, adults grow to weigh between 60 and 120 pounds (27 and 54 kilograms).

Fast Facts about Afghanistan's History

Year of founding: 1747
Founder: Ahmad Shah
Year of independence: 1919 (from the United Kingdom)
National holiday: August 19
Current type of government: Interim Administration
Head of government: president

Chapter 3

Afghanistan's History and Government

People have lived in Afghanistan for more than 50,000 years. Scientists have discovered the remains of wild types of wheat there. This wheat shows that the country had one of the earliest societies to grow crops.

Early Civilizations

Between 2000 and 1500 B.C., Aryans moved south from Central Asia into Iran, Afghanistan, and India. The Indo-Aryan language spoken by these people developed into the modern languages spoken in Iran, Afghanistan, Pakistan, and India.

The Persian Empire took over Afghanistan around 500 B.C. The Persians were nomads from present-day Russia who began to move into the area in 1000 B.C. They eventually ruled a large empire that extended from Egypt to India. The Persians ruled from an area called Persia in present-day Iran.

◀ Sculptures of warriors adorn the Audience Hall in Persepolis, Iran, built by Persian King Darius I in the 400s B.C.

When Alexander the Great invaded Persia around 330 B.C., Afghanistan became part of the Greek Empire. Alexander's empire was divided between several of his generals after his death in 323 B.C. Without a strong central authority, the empire weakened. The Mauryan Empire from northern India took over areas of the Hindu Kush Mountains. The Mauryans brought Buddhism to parts of Afghanistan.

The Kushans and the Arabs

Control of Afghanistan passed through several more rulers before the Kushans gained control of the area in 135 B.C. The Kushans were Buddhists. They carved huge statues of Buddha into the mountains of central Afghanistan. During this empire, Afghanistan became part of the Silk Road between China and Rome. Merchants from China, India, and Rome traded fabrics, jewelry, spices, and carved ivory along this trade route.

Several more groups gained control of Afghanistan after the Kushans, but the Arabs were the most influential. They began to invade the area in A.D. 642 and had control of Afghanistan by 714. They brought the religion of Islam, which spread rapidly across Afghanistan. Islam continues to influence Afghanistan's government today.

▲ The Kushan Buddha statue in this photo was destroyed by Afghanistan's Taliban government in 2001.

Turks and Mongols

Muslim Turks invaded present-day Afghanistan in 999. An important leader during this time was Mahmud of Ghazni. Art and learning thrived during his reign. He ruled an empire that stretched from Kabul to India.

Mongols, led by Genghis Khan, invaded the area from Mongolia in 1219. The Mongols destroyed entire

cities in their conquest. Genghis Khan tried to destroy Islamic religion and culture but did not succeed.

In the late 1200s, Italian Marco Polo traveled through Afghanistan on his way to China. He wrote about the Mongol empire in his book *Description of the World*, finished in 1298.

By 1370, Timur, another Mongol from Asia, had taken control of present-day Afghanistan. Timur built a Muslim empire and ruled until the early 1400s.

Over the next 300 years, many people ruled Afghanistan. One of the most important was Babur, a Muslim who founded the Mogul Empire in 1526. This empire was originally based in Kabul, but Babur later moved to Delhi in India to rule his huge empire.

After Babur's death, Afghanistan became caught in a tug-of-war between the Mogul Empire and the Safavid dynasty of Persia. For 200 years, these two powers fought over the land. The Persian king Nadir Shah eventually defeated the Mogul Empire in 1739.

The Kingdom of Afghanistan

Ahmad Khan was the leader of Nadir Shah's personal bodyguards and an Afghan. He belonged to the powerful Pashtun tribe. When Nadir Shah was killed in 1747, Ahmad Khan fled to Afghanistan. He saw

◀ Babur holds a bird on his hand in this illustration from the *Baburnama*, a book about the life of Babur written only a few decades after his death.

an opportunity for the Afghan people to break away from Persia.

Ahmad Khan met with other tribal leaders near Kandahar. In October 1747, the tribal leaders declared him the king of Afghanistan. He renamed himself shah, the Persian word for king. He founded a capital city at Kandahar and then set out to conquer India.

By 1761, the Kingdom of Afghanistan reached from the Amu Darya River in the north to the Indian Ocean in the south. It also reached from western Iran to the Indus River in Pakistan. Throughout his life, Ahmad Shah fought to expand his kingdom. He also fought many battles to maintain control of the different tribes within its borders. Ahmad Shah died in 1773.

Ahmad Shah's heirs to the throne were eventually defeated by a rival tribe led by Dost Muhammad in 1826. Dost Muhammad Shah ruled during a time of British and Russian fighting that would take its toll on Afghanistan.

The Anglo-Afghan Wars

By the early 1800s, both Great Britain and Russia became interested in Afghanistan. Great Britain was afraid that Russia would invade British India by traveling across Afghanistan. Russia wanted a southern route to the sea. In 1809, Afghanistan signed a treaty

◀ Dost Muhammad Shah took over rule of Afghanistan in 1826.

with Great Britain to keep Russians from traveling through Afghanistan.

In 1837, Persia invaded western Afghanistan. Russia supported Persia. The British allied with the Afghans in Herat, Kabul, and Kandahar. The Afghan leader Dost Muhammad asked the British to help him regain territory near Peshawar. The British refused. Dost Muhammad decided to see if the

▼ The British defend a fort outside Kabul during the Second Anglo-Afghan War.

Russians would help him. Since Britain did not want Russia in Afghanistan, the British invaded Afghanistan to keep the Russians out. Britain's invasion started the First Anglo-Afghan War (1839–1842).

The British captured Kabul, and Dost Muhammad fled to northern Afghanistan. The Afghans soon rebelled against Great Britain. In October 1842, the British finally left Afghanistan. Dost Muhammad returned to lead Afghanistan and began to unite the different regions. When he died in 1863, his son Sher Ali became leader.

In 1878, Sher Ali met with Russian diplomats in Kabul. The British sent a group of diplomats too, but Sher Ali refused to meet with them. The British returned with 40,000 soldiers, and the Second Anglo-Afghan War (1878–1880) began. At the end of the war, the Afghans agreed to allow Great Britain to handle their relationships with other countries.

In 1893, the British set the modern borders of Afghanistan with the Durand Agreement. This border divided the land of the Pashtun tribes of eastern Afghanistan and modern Pakistan. It was not a popular decision with the tribes.

Independent Afghanistan

In 1919, Afghanistan's ruler, Amanullah Khan, attacked India, a colony of the United Kingdom, to gain independence from the United Kingdom. This short battle became known as the Third Anglo-Afghan War (1919). In the Treaty of Rawalpindi, the United Kingdom agreed to give Afghanistan complete independence.

Amanullah declared himself king and introduced Afghanistan's first constitution. The constitution created courts, laws, and a legislature to replace the traditional tribal government. These changes upset the traditional tribal leaders and religious leadership. They rebelled against the aggressive modern ideas Amanullah proposed. They forced Amanullah to leave the country in 1929. The tribes elected Mohammad Nadir as shah in 1929. His government was based on traditional Islamic laws.

In 1933, Mohammad Nadir was killed, and his son Zahir became shah. From 1933 until 1973, Afghanistan began to build its education systems and industry. Northwestern farmers exported the famous karakul lambskins. Kabul University was created in 1946.

Communism and the Soviet Union

Afghanistan's many tribal groups could not agree on a government. Some wanted a democracy, while others wanted a communist government. Still others wanted a traditional Islamic government.

In 1973, Mohammad Daoud and the military, helped by the Soviet Union, overthrew Zahir Shah. Daoud declared the new Republic of Afghanistan. In 1978, leaders of the People's Democratic Party killed Daoud and formed a new communist government. Communism is a way of organizing a country so all land, money, and industry belong to the people but are administered by the government.

▲ Mujahideen stand atop a crashed Soviet helicopter during the Soviet invasion.

In 1979, the Soviet Union invaded Afghanistan to help keep the communist government in control. At the same time, traditional Afghan tribes formed an army to overthrow the government. These fighters are known as the mujahideen (moo-ha-hi-DEEN). It means "defenders of Islam" in Arabic. The United

States, Saudi Arabia, and Pakistan supplied weapons and training to the mujahideen. The Soviets were never able to conquer these determined fighters.

In 1988, the United Nations brought Afghanistan, Pakistan, the Soviet Union, and the United States together to discuss peace. They signed an agreement that required the Soviet Union to withdraw from Afghanistan. The last Soviet soldier left Afghanistan in February 1989. Nearly 15,000 Soviet soldiers were killed. But more than 1 million Afghans were killed between 1979 and 1989.

Civil War and the Taliban

Civil war broke out in Afghanistan after the Soviets left. The mujahideen represented many tribes and ethnic groups with different ideas of what form the government should take. In 1996, a group called the Taliban took over. Taliban means "religious students." They wanted to give Afghanistan an ultra-orthodox system of Islamic laws and government. By 1998, the Taliban controlled 90 percent of the country. Though they stopped much of the fighting, they were still at war with a group of mujahideen called the Northern Alliance.

The Taliban passed ultra-orthodox Islamic laws. This form of Islam was in conflict with the moderate

▼ A young Taliban guard waits at his post outside a city.

form of Islam practiced by most Afghans. Men were expected to pray five times a day and to grow their beards. Women could not work outside their homes. They were required to wear a veil and be escorted by a male relative when they went out. Girls were forbidden to attend school. The government strictly enforced the rules. If women did not wear a veil, they were beaten.

> **Did you know...?**
> Experts estimate that 10 million land mines are left in Afghanistan after the wars. These land mines kill or hurt an average of three people every day.

The Taliban also welcomed Osama bin Laden, a Saudi Arabian. He had helped the mujahideen with money, weapons, and men in the war against the Soviet Union. The Taliban allowed bin Laden to set up camps that trained men for a war against his enemies. Bin Laden gave the Taliban money and support for their new government. Both the Taliban and bin Laden believed in very strict interpretations of Islamic laws and customs.

Fall of the Taliban

On September 11, 2001, the United States was attacked by a terrorist group called Al-Qaida. This group trained with bin Laden in Afghanistan. The United States asked the Taliban to turn over bin Laden and his followers for trial. The Taliban refused. As a result, the United States attacked bin Laden and Al-Qaida in Afghanistan. Other Afghan tribes joined the United States to force the Taliban to surrender. By November 2001, the Taliban surrendered Kabul and Kandahar and fled into the mountains.

In December 2001, members of the many tribes and political groups in Afghanistan met in Germany

▲ U.S. troops check caves during the search for Al-Qaida members in 2001–2002.

to discuss a new government for Afghanistan. They agreed that a traditional Loya Jirga, or Grand Council, should be called to decide the future government and leaders of Afghanistan. The United Nations promised millions of dollars to help Afghanistan recover from the destruction of its land, economy, and natural resources that resulted from the wars.

Afghanistan's Government

A Loya Jirga representing all Afghans met in June 2002. The council drew 1,650 Afghans to elect a new president, plan a temporary government, and name important new ministers. The temporary government is called the Interim Administration. It will govern Afghanistan for 18 months.

The Loya Jirga elected Hamid Karzai as the president of the Interim Administration. Karzai appointed a group of people to advise him. These ministers will take charge of national defense, women's affairs, health, education, aviation, and tourism. Karzai tried to include women and many Afghan ethnic groups when he named these ministers. Women were chosen to lead the departments of health and women's affairs.

Karzai said he wants to build peace among the different tribes and oversee the writing of a new constitution. Most important, Karzai must find the money to develop agriculture, mineral resources, and trade to restart Afghanistan's economy.

In June 2004, another Loya Jirga is planned. Afghans will then vote on a new constitution and hold democratic elections for the new leaders of Afghanistan.

◀ Hamid Karzai votes during the elections for the Interim Administration, in which he won the office of president.

Fast Facts about Afghanistan's Economy

Major natural resources: natural gas, coal, copper, iron ore
Major agricultural products: wheat, fruits, nuts, cotton, wool
Major manufactured products: cotton textiles, soap, shoes, fertilizer, handwoven carpets
Major imports: oil, food, machinery
Major exports: natural gas, fruits, wool, cotton, gemstones

Chapter 4

Afghanistan's Economy

Afghanistan has never been a wealthy country. Before the Soviet war, 85 percent of Afghans were farmers. They raised enough food to feed themselves, their families, and their animals. Extra grain, milk, or meat could be traded for what farmers could not grow. Wars further weakened the economy, destroying roads and making shipping unsafe.

Agriculture

Most Afghan farmers raise a few animals for their own needs. Cattle supply 70 percent of the milk, and sheep and goats provide the rest. Some nomads raise large herds of sheep and goats. They move their herds to mountain grasslands in the spring. Besides milk, sheep and goats provide wool and meat. Other farmers raise horses, camels, and donkeys to use for transportation.

◀ Afghan nomads herd their sheep near water during a fall migration to a new grazing area.

Afghanistan's mountains and dry climate leave little good land for crop farming. Only 12 percent of the land is good for growing crops. Most successful farms are in the northern plains. Still, farmers there depend on the rivers to irrigate their fields. The Afghans developed a system of ditches to bring water from the rivers to their fields. The primary crop is wheat. Before the Soviet war, more than 80 percent of the wheat was grown on irrigated lands. Corn, barley, cotton, rice, and sugarcane are also grown.

Along the Kabul and Arghandab Rivers in eastern and southeastern Afghanistan, orchards produce a good variety of fruits and nuts. Apples, pears, peaches, plums, grapes, and cherries are grown in this area. Orchards also produce almonds, pistachios, and walnuts. These fruits and nuts provide a good source of income for merchants who sell them in markets in Pakistan and India.

Afghanistan is also a major grower of opium poppies. The seeds of these plants are used to make the illegal drug heroin. Although it is illegal to grow opium poppies in Afghanistan, the government does not have enough money or police to enforce the laws. Farmers grow the illegal plants because opium brings them much more money than legal crops.

Natural Resources

The mountains of Afghanistan hold a wealth of natural resources, but the country lacks the money to

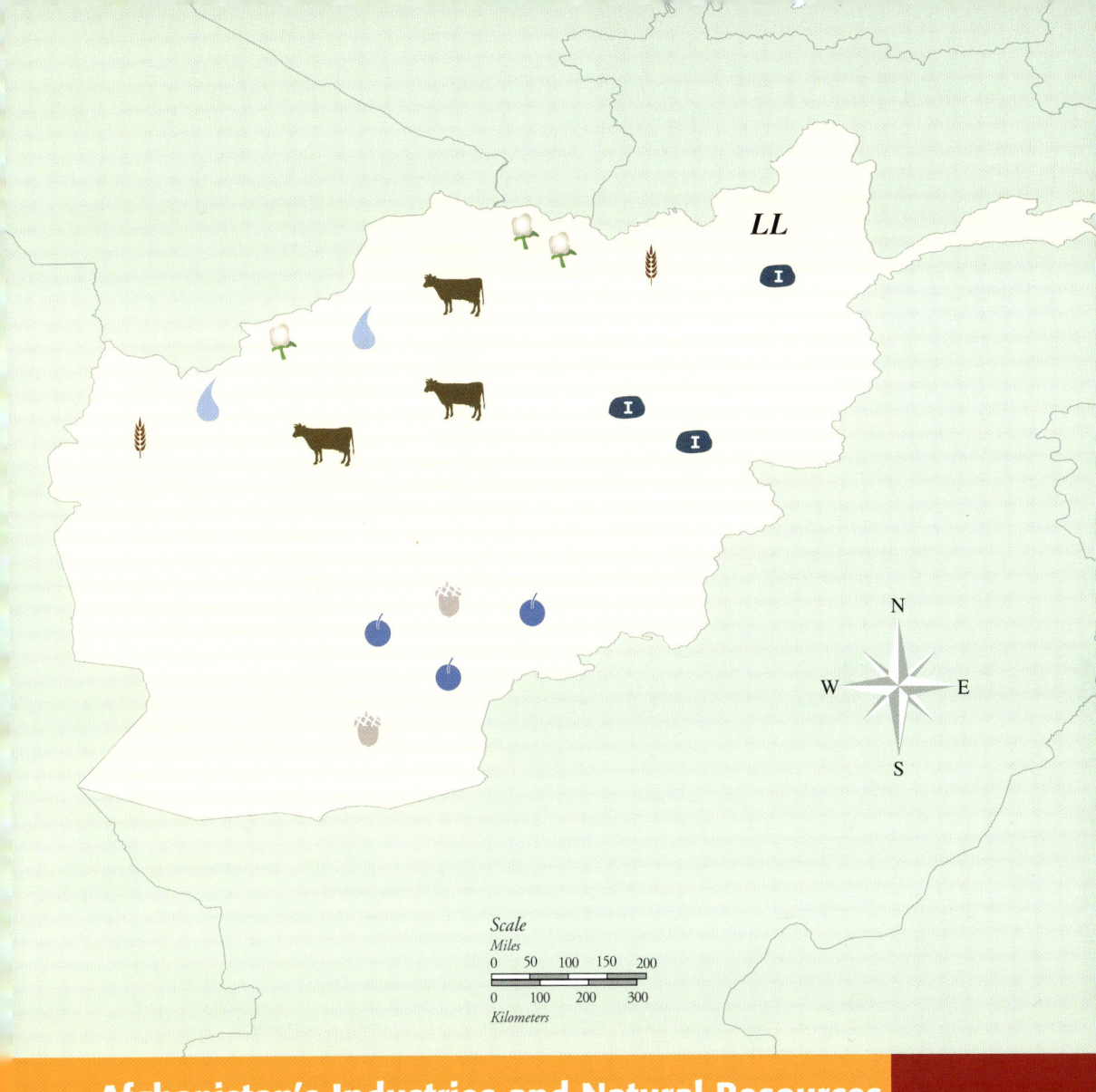

Afghanistan's Industries and Natural Resources

KEY
- cotton
- fruits
- iron
- lapis lazuli
- livestock
- natural gas
- nuts
- wheat

39

Afghanistan's Money

Afghanistan distributed new paper currency in October 2002. The name of the currency is the same as the previous currency—the Afghani. One Afghani is divided into 100 puls. New coins will be minted sometime in the future.

Exchange rates can change daily. In early 2003, 1 U.S. dollar equaled 43 Afghanis, and 1 Canadian dollar equaled 29 Afghanis.

100 Afghani note

10 Afghani note

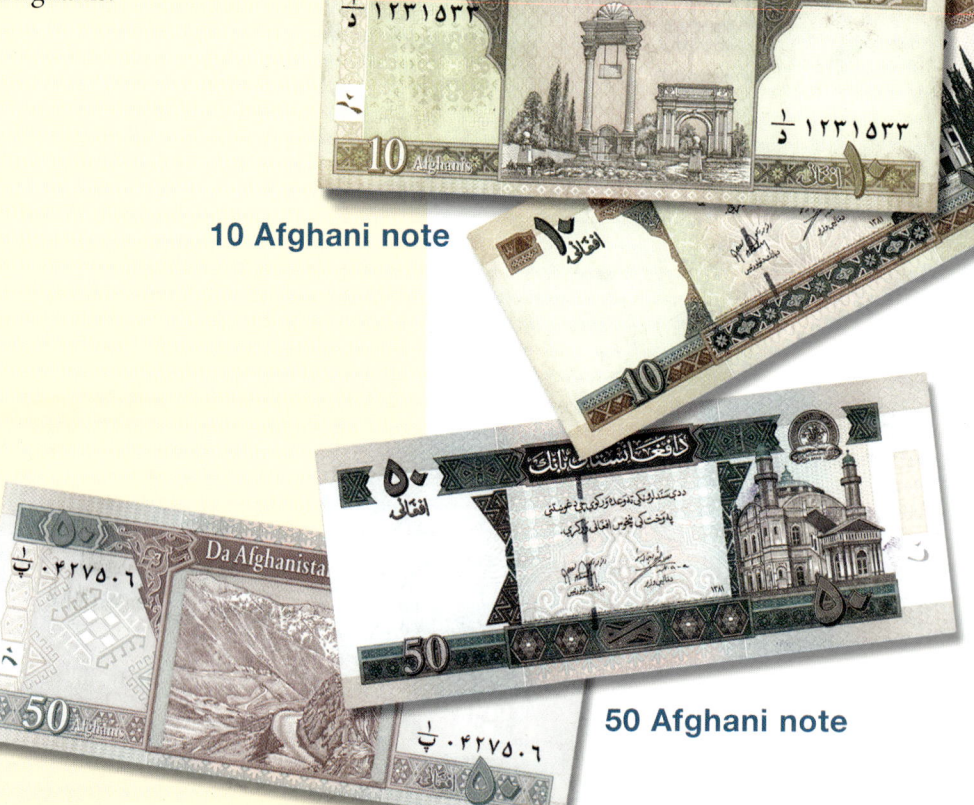

50 Afghani note

develop the mines. Deposits of coal, copper, silver, and gold have been found. Afghanistan is also believed to have large deposits of iron ore.

Gemstones are also found in Afghanistan's mountains. Deposits of emeralds, rubies, and lapis lazuli are mined. Lapis lazuli is a gemstone found in only three places in the world. The color ranges from deep blue to light blue or green. The most valuable lapis lazuli is dark blue. Afghans have mined this gem for more than 6,000 years.

Natural gas is one of the country's resources that has been tapped. Large deposits are found beneath the northern plains. Pipelines have been damaged in the wars, but gas will be an important export when the pipelines are repaired.

Energy and Transportation

Reliable sources of energy are needed to develop Afghanistan's industries. In the past, Afghanistan dammed rivers to produce hydroelectricity. This electricity is available only in the major cities. The majority of Afghans live in small villages throughout the countryside without electricity. They use wood and dung to build fires to heat their homes and cook food.

Other than a few paved roads that run between major cities, most of the country's roads are dirt. In

> **Did you know...?**
> In Afghanistan in 2002, a good camel typically cost about U.S. $500.

the large cities, buses, cars, and bicycles are common types of transportation. Colorfully painted trucks transport goods and people between cities. In rural areas, horses, donkeys, and camels are better transportation than cars or buses.

Rebuilding

Afghans face great challenges to rebuild their economy. First, the government must make sure people are safe so they can begin rebuilding. Both businesses and farmers need good roads to bring their products to market. Farmers will need seeds, tools, livestock, and repaired irrigation systems. Planting new trees will protect the soil and provide firewood. The Afghans are willing to work hard to rebuild their farms, villages, and cities.

Many people in Afghanistan work in jobs that are considered part of the informal economy. They are not registered with the government, but they make money at jobs. Some of these people sell items at markets and roadside stands, drive taxis, or perform services.

Afghanistan has the potential to have a thriving economy. Even after years of war, Afghan handmade carpets are known all around the world. Their lapis lazuli is the best available. Karakul sheep produce some of the softest wool in the world. With the help of other countries, the Afghans can begin to grow the economy.

▼ Many people in Afghanistan sell items at roadside stands or markets.

Fast Facts about Afghanistan's People

Population distribution: urban—30 percent; rural—70 percent
Official languages: Pashto and Dari
Population growth rate: 3.43 percent (includes returning refugees)
Life expectancy: 47 years; male—47 years, female—46 years
Literacy rate: 36 percent of Afghans older than age 15 can read and write

Chapter 5

Afghanistan's People, Culture, and Daily Life

Afghanistan has been an Asian crossroads since the beginning of its history. For thousands of years, waves of merchants and invaders crossed this rugged land. All of them left something behind in Afghanistan. The diverse tribes, customs, and languages in Afghanistan today reflect its history of invasion.

Major Ethnic Groups

Afghanistan's geography physically separates the largest ethnic groups. The largest group, the Pashtuns, live east and south of the central highlands. They speak Pashto. They grow crops and raise livestock. Most of Afghanistan's nomads are Pashtuns. The name "Afghan" was originally given to the Pashtun people, but it now applies to all people in Afghanistan.

The northern plains are home to the Tajiks, the second largest ethnic group. They speak Dari. The

◀ Afghanistan's people reflect the diverse cultures that have come through Afghanistan over the centuries.

Tajiks see themselves as members of a specific home region or valley. Many Tajiks also live in Kabul.

The middle of the central highlands is called the Land of the Hazara because it is the traditional home of the Hazara people. They speak Hazaragi, a Persian language with some Mongol words. In the 1960s, many Hazara migrated to the cities to find work.

Cities and Villages

In the 1960s, the government began to build a system of paved roads between major Afghan cities. The cities were usually located near major crossroads or rivers. When travel became easier, more people moved to the cities to find jobs. During times of war, many rural Afghans moved to the cities to avoid the fighting. Today, cities are unable to provide housing, clean water, and electricity for all the refugees from the wars.

Rural Afghans live in homes built from bricks. Often, a tall stone wall encloses the house and a courtyard. The walls provide privacy. In some areas, the houses have flat roofs that are used for drying vegetables and for sleeping during hot summer nights. Several related families might share these homes. Water is drawn from nearby pools and rivers.

Nomads make up a small part of the population. In the past, nomads lived in tents near their herds of

▼ Buildings in Kabul in 2002 show the destruction of the recent wars.

sheep. Today, many live in houses most of the year. About 80 percent of the nomads are Pashtuns.

Religion and Holidays

One unifying force in Afghanistan is the religion of Islam. Nearly all Afghans are Muslim. About 84 percent are Sunni Muslims, and about 15 percent

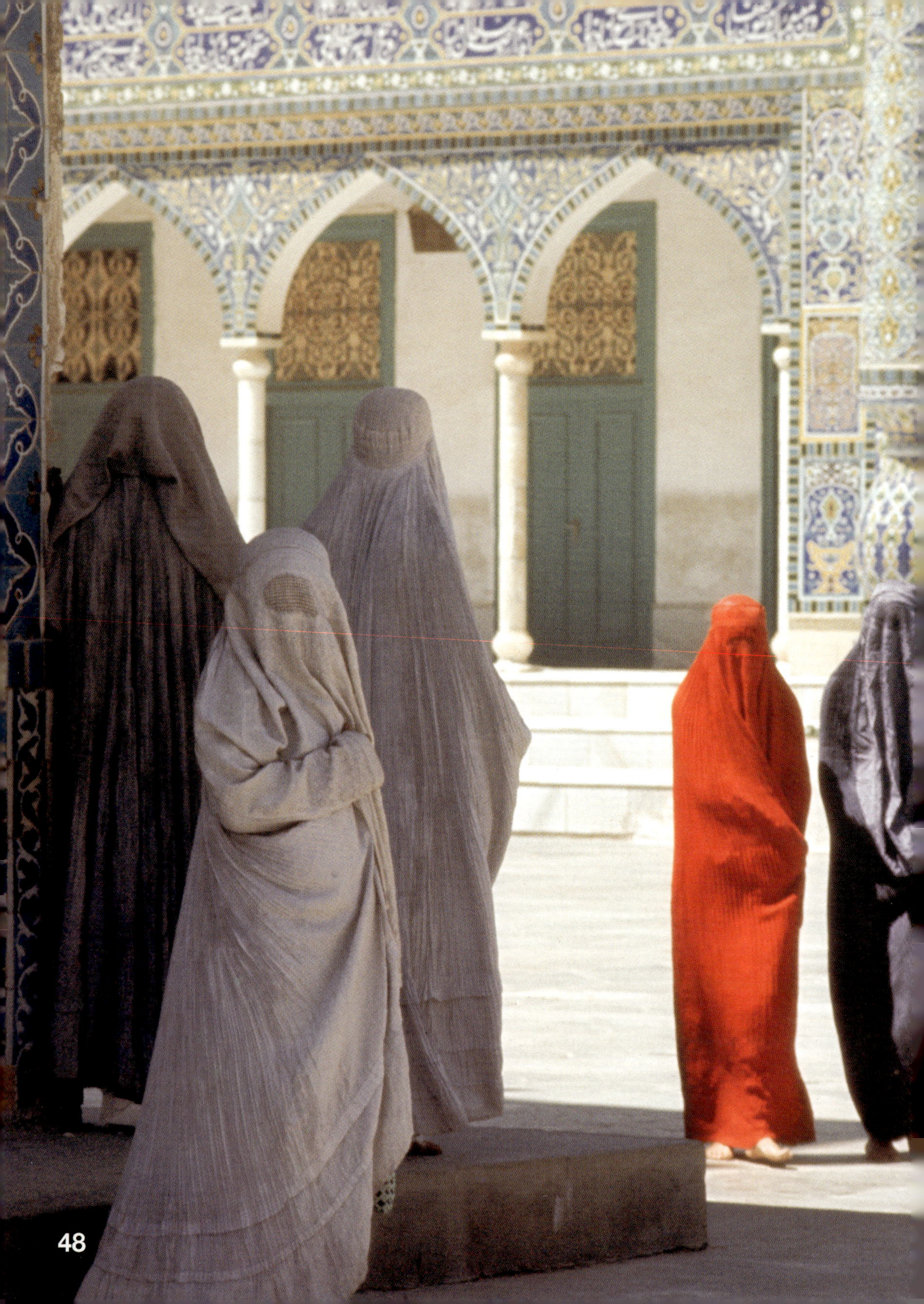

are Shiite Muslims. Islam encourages generosity, fairness, honesty, tolerance, and respect for the community. Religion affects the government, the schools, and the everyday life of the Afghans.

Most Afghan holidays celebrate Islam's holy days. The ninth month of the Islamic calendar is called Ramadan. The Islamic calendar is a lunar calendar, so Ramadan starts on a different date each year. During Ramadan, all Muslims except the old, the sick, young children, and pregnant women fast from dawn to dusk. They do not eat or drink during these hours. The fast helps Muslims remember their duty to Allah. After dusk, families gather together to eat a large meal.

At the end of Ramadan, the feast of Eid al-Fitr takes place. This celebration lasts about three days. Afghans go to the mosque, prepare special meals, and visit with friends.

Women in Afghanistan

The Taliban placed harsh restrictions on education, work, and health care for women. These restrictions have changed. Women and girls may now go back to school and work. Afghanistan is changing once again, as it has changed many times in the past.

Women in Afghanistan's multi-ethnic society follow a wide range of customs. In cities, some women still wear a head-to-toe veil called a chadari when they leave the house. In very strict Muslim families, women never

◀ Women at a mosque in Mazar-e Sharif wear chadaris. Some women still wear chadaris when they leave the house.

leave the house. Their role is to take care of their family, prepare food, and clean the house. Children fetch water for them. Men go out to work and to shop.

Some urban and many rural women do not follow such strict rules. Women often cover their heads and faces, but they usually do not wear a chadari. Rural women and men split the work of farming and caring for livestock.

Education

It has not been easy for most people to get an education in Afghanistan. In 1935, the Afghan government declared that elementary education would be free and required for all Afghans. But before the war began in 1979, only large cities and towns had school buildings and teachers. When the Taliban took over in 1996, women were no longer allowed to teach or attend school. Schools no longer had enough teachers. Today, Afghanistan has one of the lowest literacy rates in the world.

Since the Taliban were removed from power, Afghan children are eager to go to school. Many women have returned to teaching. In February 2002, Ariana Afghan High School reopened in Kabul. More than 500 girls were immediately enrolled, and 200 more waited to register.

Many children learn to read and write Pashto in school. In this school, boys and girls attend class together. ▶

Learn to Speak Pashto

Many ethnic groups live in Afghanistan. Afghanistan has more than 70 languages and dialects. Pashto and Dari are the two official languages. They are written in Arabic script, which is unlike the English alphabet. Below, some helpful Pashto words are written in the English alphabet.

hello—assalam u alaikum (ah-sah-LAM OO ah-LEHK-uhm)

good-bye—de kuday pe aman (DU KOO-day POO AHM-ahn)

please—lutfan (LOOT-fahn)

thank you—sta na shukria (STAH NAH SHOO-kree-uh)

Do you speak English?—Ta pe angrezai pohegy? (TAH POO ahn-GROO-zay PO-hug-ee?)

> **Did you know...?**
> Most Muslims follow dietary laws. Certain food and drink is forbidden, or "haram." Alcohol and pork are two haram items.

Afghanistan still greatly lacks desks, books, and other resources. The government has not yet been able to provide schools in much of Afghanistan. In these areas, the village mullah, or priest, often teaches children at the mosque. These children usually learn to read from the Qu'ran, the holy book of Islam.

Food

Afghans have a variety of foods to choose from. Almost everyone eats flat bread called naan. Cooks make pilau, a mixture of rice and vegetables or meat. They might serve squash, carrots, eggplants, spinach, or potatoes with the pilau. Meat is often roasted on skewers called kebabs. Meat from sheep, called mutton, is most commonly eaten. Rural families depend on the fresh fruits and vegetables available at the weekly market if they do not raise their own.

Cities have a larger variety of food and vegetables available year round. Afghans remember more than 100 kinds of fruits and vegetables in the markets before the war with the Soviet Union.

Dairy products are also important. Many Afghans drink cow, goat, or sheep milk or buttermilk. Yogurt and cheese are also available.

Make Khatai Cookies

Pistachios are native to the mountains of Afghanistan. They are grown in areas of the northern plains and the river valleys of Kabul and Kandahar. These nuts are found in many dishes, including puddings and desserts.

What You Need

Ingredients
1½ cups (360 mL) white flour
1 cup (240 mL) sugar
1 tablespoon (15 mL) crushed cardamon
¾ cup (175 mL) corn oil
½ cup (120 mL) ground pistachio nuts

Equipment
medium bowl
dry-ingredient measuring cups
liquid-ingredient measuring cup
mixing spoon
baking sheet
flat-bottomed drinking glass
potholders
spatula

What You Do

1. Preheat the oven to 350°F (180°C).
2. Mix the flour, the sugar, and the cardamon in a medium bowl.
3. Next, add the corn oil and mix well.
4. Roll pieces of the dough into 1-inch (2.5-centimeter) round balls.
5. Roll each ball in the ground pistachio nuts and place them on a baking sheet about 2 inches (5 centimeters) apart.
6. Use a flat-bottomed drinking glass to flatten each dough ball.
7. Bake for 15 minutes, or until light brown.
8. Remove cookies from oven with potholders and allow to cool completely.
9. Remove from sheet with a spatula. Cookies will be crumbly.

Makes about 2 dozen cookies

Leisure and Sports

Afghan children play many games. Soccer, tag, and hopscotch are very popular. Kite flying is popular with children and adults.

Music is a popular form of entertainment, especially in rural areas. People often sing at special events or get-togethers.

Cock fighting is another sport that interests adults. Gamecocks look like roosters. Two gamecocks are put in a ring and fight each other. Fans bet on the winner of these matches.

The game of buzkashi is a traditional game often played in northern Afghanistan where horses are an integral part of life and culture. Buzkashi means "goat killing." Players on horseback try to pick up a dead, headless goat or calf from a circle drawn on the field. The player then carries the calf to a point 1 mile (1.6 kilometers) away and returns it to the circle. When he drops the calf in the circle, he has scored a goal.

Teams can have as many as 100 players. Each team tries to keep the other team away from the calf. Players cannot hit each other on the hand, trip a horse, or tie the calf to their saddles. The riders are experts, the horses are well trained, and large crowds come out to watch this fast, exciting game. It is traditional to play buzkashi at weddings in the northern part of the country.

▲ Players try to steal the calf in a fast-paced game of buzkashi in 2002.

▲ The minaret at Ghazni was once part of a mosque. It was built in the A.D. 1100s.

Afghanistan's National Symbols

◀ Afghanistan's Flag

In January 2002, the Interim Administration adopted a new flag for Afghanistan. It is similar to the flag of the Kingdom of Afghanistan, which was overthrown in 1973. The new flag will have a black stripe that represents the past wars. The red stripe represents the blood of Afghan's freedom fighters. The green stripe represents peace and is a color associated with Islam. Afghanistan's seal lies in the center.

◀ Afghanistan's Great Seal

Afghanistan's Great Seal shows a mosque where people pray and the pulpit from which religious leaders address the followers. There are flags on each side of the mosque. The mosque is ringed with sheaves of wheat, a major crop of Afghanistan.

National anthem: "Sorode Meli" ("National Anthem")

57

Timeline

330-323 B.C. Alexander the Great makes Afghanistan part of the Greek Empire.

1219 Genghis Khan invades Afghanistan.

1747 Ahmad Shah founds the Kingdom of Afghanistan.

1878-1880 The Second Anglo-Afghan War takes place; Afghanistan lets Britain set foreign policy.

B.C.   A.D.   1200   1800

500 B.C. Afghanistan is part of the Persian Empire.

A.D. 642 Arabs invade Afghanistan and introduce Islam.

1526 Babur takes control of Kabul and establishes the Mogul Empire.

1839-1842 The First Anglo-Afghan War takes place.

1893 The British divide Afghanistan and Pakistan with the Durand Line.

1919
The Third Anglo-Afghan War occurs; Afghanistan becomes independent of Great Britain.

1973
Daoud overthrows Zahir Shah; Republic of Afghanistan is created.

1989
The Soviet Union leaves Afghanistan.

2001
The United States forces the Taliban out of Afghanistan.

1900

2000

1933
Zahir Shah becomes Afghanistan's ruler.

1979
The Soviet Union invades and occupies Afghanistan.

1996
The Taliban take over Afghanistan.

2002
Hamid Karzai is elected president of the new Interim Administration.

59

Words to Know

chadari (SHAH-duh-ree)—a long veil that covers the body

communism (KOM-yoo-niz-uhm)—a way of organizing a country so the land, houses, and businesses are owned by all but administered by the government

conquer (KONG-kur)—to defeat an enemy and take over

deposit (di-POZ-it)—natural layer of minerals in the earth

ethnic (ETH-nik)—related to a group of people and their culture

interim (IN-tuh-rim)—temporary

karakul (KAH-rah-kool)—type of sheep, also called Persian lamb

nomad (NOH-mad)—a person who moves from place to place to find food and water, rather than living in one spot

orthodox (OR-thuh-doks)—belief in older, strict interpretations of a religion's teachings

refugee (REF-yuh-jee)—a person forced to leave his or her home because of war

shah (SHAW)—Persian word for king

Taliban (TAHL-ee-bahn)—religious students; a group of these students took control of Afghanistan in 1996.

To Learn More

Banting, Erinn. *Afghanistan. The People.* Lands, Peoples, and Cultures. New York: Crabtree, 2003.

Corona, Laurel. *Afghanistan.* Modern Nations of the World. San Diego: Lucent Books, 2002.

Greenblatt, Miriam. *Afghanistan.* Enchantment of the World. Second Series. New York: Children's Press, 2003.

Gritzner, Jeffrey. *Afghanistan.* Modern World Nations. Philadelphia: Chelsea House, 2002.

Gunderson, Cory Gideon. *Afghanistan's Struggles.* World in Conflict—the Middle East. Edina, Minn.: Abdo, 2003.

Kazem, Halima. *Afghanistan.* Countries of the World. Milwaukee: Gareth Stevens, 2003.

Useful Addresses

Consulate-General of Afghanistan in New York
360 Lexington Avenue, 11th Floor
New York, NY 10017

Embassy of Afghanistan
2000 L Street NW
Suite 200
Washington, DC 20036

Internet Sites

Do you want to learn more about Afghanistan?
Visit the FactHound at *http://www.facthound.com*

FactHound can track down many sites to help you. All the FactHound sites are hand-selected by our editors. FactHound will fetch the best, most accurate information to answer your questions.

IT'S EASY! IT'S FUN!
1) Go to *http://www.facthound.com*
2) Type in: 0736821740
3) Click on "FETCH IT" and FactHound will put you on the trail of several helpful links.

You can also search by subject or book title. So, relax and let our pal FactHound do the research for you!

▲ Children play with balloons bought from a street vendor. Balloons were banned under the Taliban's rule.

Index

agriculture, 9, 11, 28, 35, 37–38, 42, 50
Ahmad Khan (Shah), 23–24
Alexander the Great, 20
Al-Qaida, 32, 33
Amanullah Khan, 27–28
Amu Darya River, 6, 9, 14, 24
Anglo-Afghan Wars, 24–27
animals. See wildlife
Arabs, 20
Aryans, 19

Babur, 23
Band-e Amir Lakes, 10
bin Laden, Osama, 32
Buddhism, 20
buzkashi, 54, 55

climate, 13–14, 38
communism, 6, 28
constitution, 27, 35

Daoud, Mohammad, 28
desert, 13, 14
Dost Muhammad Shah, 24, 25, 26
Durand Agreement, 27

earthquakes, 11
education, 28, 31, 35, 49, 50, 52
energy, 41

farming. See agriculture
flag, 57
food, 16, 37, 41, 50, 52, 53

Genghis Khan, 21, 23
Great Britain, 24–27

Hazara, 46
Helmand River, 10, 13
heroin, 38

Hindu Kush Mountains, 10, 20
holidays, 49

Interim Administration, 35, 57
irrigation, 9, 38, 42
Islam, 20, 23, 28, 29, 30, 31, 32, 47, 49, 52, 57

Kabul, 5, 10, 13–14, 21, 23, 25, 26, 27, 32, 46, 47, 50
Kabul River, 10, 38
Kandahar, 13, 24, 25, 32
Karzai, Hamid, 35
Khyber Pass, 5–6
Kushans, 20, 21

lapis lazuli, 41, 42
livestock, 9, 37, 42, 45, 50
Loya Jirga, 33, 35

Mahmud of Ghazni, 21
Mauryan Empire, 20
Mazar-e Sharif, 10, 13, 49
Mogul Empire, 23
Mongols, 21, 23
mujahideen, 29–30, 32

Nadir, Mohammad, 28
Nadir Shah, 23
natural gas, 41
natural resources, 33, 38, 39, 41
nomads, 12, 19, 37, 45, 46–47
Northern Alliance, 30

Pakistan, 5, 6, 10, 19, 24, 27, 30, 38
Pashtuns, 23, 27, 45, 47
Persian Empire, 19, 23, 24, 25
plant life, 14, 16, 38, 42
Polo, Marco, 23
precipitation, 9, 13, 14

refugees, 14, 46
religion, 20, 23, 47, 49
Russia, 19, 24–27. See also Soviet Union

seal, 57
Silk Road, 20
Sistan Basin, 13
Soviet Union, 6, 28, 29–30, 32, 52
sports, 54

Tajiks, 45–46
Taliban, 6, 30–31, 32, 50, 63
temperature, 13–14
Timur, 23
transportation, 37, 41–42
Treaty of Rawalpindi, 27

United States, 6, 29–30, 32, 33

wheat, 19, 38, 57
wildlife, 14, 16, 17
women, 31, 35, 49–50

Zahir Shah, 28

64